50 Milk Making Recipes for Home

By: Kelly Johnson

Table of Contents

- Lactation Cookies
- Oatmeal with Almonds and Flaxseed
- Spinach and Banana Smoothie
- Garlic Parmesan Lactation Breadsticks
- Brewer's Yeast Banana Bread
- Quinoa Salad with Kale and Cranberries
- Carrot and Ginger Lactation Muffins
- Spinach and Mushroom Frittata
- Lentil Soup with Barley and Kale
- Oatmeal Chocolate Chip Lactation Bars
- Almond Butter Banana Smoothie
- Sweet Potato and Lentil Curry
- Blueberry Lactation Pancakes
- Salmon and Spinach Omelette
- Pumpkin Spice Lactation Muffins
- Spinach and Ricotta Stuffed Shells
- Apricot and Almond Lactation Bites
- Chicken and Vegetable Stir-Fry
- Raspberry Chia Seed Pudding
- Peanut Butter Lactation Energy Balls
- Vegetable and Bean Chili
- Apple Cinnamon Lactation Muffins
- Greek Yogurt Parfait with Berries
- Tofu and Vegetable Stir-Fry
- Chocolate Avocado Lactation Smoothie
- Quinoa and Black Bean Salad
- Spinach and Cheese Quesadillas
- Chickpea and Sweet Potato Curry
- Mango Coconut Lactation Popsicles
- Turkey and Vegetable Meatballs
- Blueberry Banana Lactation Smoothie
- Caprese Salad with Balsamic Glaze
- Lentil and Vegetable Soup
- Pumpkin Spice Lactation Latte
- Avocado Toast with Poached Egg

- Chicken and Broccoli Casserole
- Almond Joy Lactation Bars
- Vegetable and Lentil Curry
- Quinoa and Vegetable Stir-Fry
- Chocolate Peanut Butter Lactation Shake
- Eggplant Parmesan
- Banana Walnut Lactation Bread
- Greek Salad with Grilled Chicken
- Lentil and Spinach Salad
- Mango Pineapple Lactation Smoothie
- Tomato Basil Lactation Soup
- Turkey and Avocado Wrap
- Black Bean and Corn Salad
- Lemon Blueberry Lactation Scones
- Vegetable and Tofu Stir-Fry

Lactation Cookies

Ingredients:

- 1 cup rolled oats
- 3/4 cup whole wheat flour
- 1/4 cup brewer's yeast
- 1/2 teaspoon baking soda
- 1/2 teaspoon ground cinnamon
- 1/4 teaspoon salt
- 1/2 cup unsalted butter, softened
- 1/2 cup granulated sugar
- 1/2 cup brown sugar, packed
- 1 large egg
- 1 teaspoon vanilla extract
- 2 tablespoons flaxseed meal
- 3 tablespoons water
- 1/2 cup chocolate chips or raisins (optional)

Instructions:

1. Preheat your oven to 350°F (175°C). Line a baking sheet with parchment paper or a silicone baking mat.
2. In a small bowl, mix together the flaxseed meal and water. Let it sit for 5-10 minutes to thicken, creating a flax "egg."
3. In a medium bowl, whisk together the rolled oats, whole wheat flour, brewer's yeast, baking soda, cinnamon, and salt. Set aside.
4. In a large bowl, cream together the softened butter, granulated sugar, and brown sugar until light and fluffy.
5. Beat in the flax "egg" and vanilla extract until well combined.
6. Gradually add the dry ingredients to the wet ingredients, mixing until just combined.
7. Fold in the chocolate chips or raisins, if using.
8. Using a cookie scoop or spoon, drop rounded tablespoons of dough onto the prepared baking sheet, spacing them about 2 inches apart.
9. Gently flatten each cookie with the back of a spoon or your fingers.

10. Bake in the preheated oven for 10-12 minutes, or until the edges are lightly golden.
11. Allow the cookies to cool on the baking sheet for 5 minutes, then transfer them to a wire rack to cool completely.
12. Store the lactation cookies in an airtight container at room temperature for up to 1 week, or freeze for longer storage.
13. Enjoy these delicious and nutritious lactation cookies as a snack to support breastfeeding!

Oatmeal with Almonds and Flaxseed

Ingredients:

- 1/2 cup rolled oats
- 1 cup water or milk (dairy or plant-based)
- 1 tablespoon flaxseed meal
- 2 tablespoons sliced almonds
- 1 tablespoon honey or maple syrup (optional)
- Pinch of cinnamon (optional)
- Fresh fruit, such as berries or sliced banana (optional)

Instructions:

1. In a small saucepan, combine the rolled oats and water or milk. Bring to a boil over medium heat.
2. Once boiling, reduce the heat to low and simmer the oats, stirring occasionally, for about 5 minutes or until they reach your desired consistency.
3. Stir in the flaxseed meal and sliced almonds, and continue to cook for another 1-2 minutes until the oats are thick and creamy.
4. If desired, sweeten the oatmeal with honey or maple syrup, and add a pinch of cinnamon for extra flavor.
5. Remove the oatmeal from the heat and let it sit for a minute or two to cool slightly.
6. Serve the oatmeal hot in a bowl, topped with fresh fruit if desired.
7. Enjoy this nutritious and filling oatmeal with almonds and flaxseed as a wholesome breakfast to start your day!

Spinach and Banana Smoothie

Ingredients:

- 1 ripe banana, peeled and sliced
- 1 cup fresh spinach leaves
- 1/2 cup plain Greek yogurt (or dairy-free yogurt for a vegan option)
- 1/2 cup milk (dairy or plant-based)
- 1 tablespoon honey or maple syrup (optional)
- 1/2 teaspoon vanilla extract
- Ice cubes (optional)

Instructions:

1. Place the banana slices, fresh spinach leaves, Greek yogurt, milk, honey or maple syrup (if using), and vanilla extract in a blender.
2. If desired, add a handful of ice cubes to the blender to make the smoothie colder and more refreshing.
3. Blend on high speed until smooth and creamy, scraping down the sides of the blender as needed to ensure all ingredients are well combined.
4. Taste the smoothie and adjust sweetness if necessary by adding more honey or maple syrup.
5. Once the smoothie reaches your desired consistency and taste, pour it into glasses and serve immediately.
6. Enjoy this nutritious and delicious spinach and banana smoothie as a refreshing breakfast or snack!

Garlic Parmesan Lactation Breadsticks

Ingredients:

- 1 1/2 cups all-purpose flour
- 1 tablespoon brewer's yeast
- 1 tablespoon flaxseed meal
- 1 tablespoon sugar
- 1 teaspoon garlic powder
- 1 teaspoon dried oregano
- 1/2 teaspoon salt
- 1/4 teaspoon black pepper
- 1/2 cup warm water
- 2 tablespoons olive oil
- 1 tablespoon grated Parmesan cheese
- 1 tablespoon melted butter
- 1 tablespoon chopped fresh parsley (optional)

Instructions:

1. Preheat your oven to 375°F (190°C). Line a baking sheet with parchment paper.
2. In a large bowl, whisk together the all-purpose flour, brewer's yeast, flaxseed meal, sugar, garlic powder, dried oregano, salt, and black pepper.
3. Gradually add the warm water and olive oil to the dry ingredients, stirring until a dough forms.
4. Turn the dough out onto a lightly floured surface and knead for 3-4 minutes, until smooth and elastic.
5. Divide the dough into 8 equal portions. Roll each portion into a long rope, about 8 inches in length.
6. Place the dough ropes on the prepared baking sheet, leaving space between each one.
7. In a small bowl, mix together the grated Parmesan cheese and melted butter. Brush the mixture over the top of each dough rope.
8. Bake in the preheated oven for 12-15 minutes, or until the breadsticks are golden brown and cooked through.
9. Remove the breadsticks from the oven and sprinkle with chopped fresh parsley, if desired.

10. Serve the garlic Parmesan lactation breadsticks warm as a delicious snack or side dish.
11. Enjoy the flavorful combination of garlic, Parmesan, and herbs in these nutritious lactation breadsticks!

Brewer's Yeast Banana Bread

Ingredients:

- 2 cups all-purpose flour
- 1/2 cup brewer's yeast
- 1/4 cup flaxseed meal
- 1 teaspoon baking powder
- 1/2 teaspoon baking soda
- 1/2 teaspoon salt
- 1/2 cup unsalted butter, melted
- 1/2 cup granulated sugar
- 1/2 cup brown sugar, packed
- 2 large eggs
- 3 ripe bananas, mashed
- 1 teaspoon vanilla extract
- 1/2 cup chopped nuts (optional)

Instructions:

1. Preheat your oven to 350°F (175°C). Grease a 9x5-inch loaf pan or line it with parchment paper.
2. In a large bowl, whisk together the all-purpose flour, brewer's yeast, flaxseed meal, baking powder, baking soda, and salt until well combined.
3. In another bowl, mix together the melted butter, granulated sugar, and brown sugar until smooth.
4. Beat in the eggs, one at a time, until well incorporated.
5. Stir in the mashed bananas and vanilla extract until combined.
6. Gradually add the dry ingredients to the wet ingredients, mixing until just combined. Be careful not to overmix.
7. If using, fold in the chopped nuts until evenly distributed throughout the batter.
8. Pour the batter into the prepared loaf pan and spread it out evenly.
9. Bake in the preheated oven for 50-60 minutes, or until a toothpick inserted into the center comes out clean.
10. Remove the banana bread from the oven and let it cool in the pan for 10 minutes before transferring it to a wire rack to cool completely.
11. Once cooled, slice and serve the Brewer's Yeast Banana Bread.
12. Enjoy this nutritious and delicious banana bread, perfect for lactating mothers!

Quinoa Salad with Kale and Cranberries

Ingredients:

- 1 cup quinoa, rinsed
- 2 cups water or vegetable broth
- 2 cups kale, stems removed and chopped
- 1/2 cup dried cranberries
- 1/4 cup sliced almonds or pecans
- 1/4 cup crumbled feta cheese (optional)
- 2 tablespoons olive oil
- 2 tablespoons lemon juice
- 1 tablespoon honey or maple syrup
- 1 teaspoon Dijon mustard
- Salt and black pepper, to taste

Instructions:

1. In a medium saucepan, combine the quinoa and water or vegetable broth. Bring to a boil over medium-high heat.
2. Reduce the heat to low, cover, and simmer for 15-20 minutes, or until the quinoa is cooked and the liquid is absorbed. Remove from heat and let it sit, covered, for 5 minutes. Fluff with a fork and let it cool.
3. In a large mixing bowl, combine the cooked quinoa, chopped kale, dried cranberries, sliced almonds or pecans, and crumbled feta cheese (if using).
4. In a small bowl, whisk together the olive oil, lemon juice, honey or maple syrup, Dijon mustard, salt, and black pepper until well combined.
5. Pour the dressing over the quinoa salad and toss until everything is evenly coated.
6. Taste and adjust seasoning, adding more salt, pepper, or lemon juice if needed.
7. Serve the quinoa salad with kale and cranberries chilled or at room temperature.
8. Enjoy this nutritious and flavorful salad as a side dish or a light meal!

Carrot and Ginger Lactation Muffins

Ingredients:

- 1 1/2 cups all-purpose flour
- 1/2 cup brewer's yeast
- 1/4 cup flaxseed meal
- 1 teaspoon baking powder
- 1/2 teaspoon baking soda
- 1/2 teaspoon salt
- 1 teaspoon ground cinnamon
- 1/2 teaspoon ground ginger
- 1/4 teaspoon ground nutmeg
- 1/2 cup unsalted butter, melted
- 1/2 cup granulated sugar
- 1/2 cup brown sugar, packed
- 2 large eggs
- 1 teaspoon vanilla extract
- 1/4 cup milk (dairy or plant-based)
- 1 1/2 cups grated carrots
- 1/4 cup chopped crystallized ginger (optional)

Instructions:

1. Preheat your oven to 350°F (175°C). Line a muffin tin with paper liners or grease it with non-stick cooking spray.
2. In a large bowl, whisk together the all-purpose flour, brewer's yeast, flaxseed meal, baking powder, baking soda, salt, ground cinnamon, ground ginger, and ground nutmeg until well combined.
3. In another bowl, mix together the melted butter, granulated sugar, and brown sugar until smooth.
4. Beat in the eggs, one at a time, until well incorporated. Stir in the vanilla extract.
5. Gradually add the dry ingredients to the wet ingredients, alternating with the milk, and mixing until just combined.
6. Fold in the grated carrots and chopped crystallized ginger (if using) until evenly distributed throughout the batter.

7. Spoon the batter into the prepared muffin tin, filling each muffin cup about 2/3 full.
8. Bake in the preheated oven for 18-20 minutes, or until a toothpick inserted into the center of a muffin comes out clean.
9. Remove the muffins from the oven and let them cool in the muffin tin for 5 minutes before transferring them to a wire rack to cool completely.
10. Once cooled, store the Carrot and Ginger Lactation Muffins in an airtight container at room temperature for up to 3 days, or freeze for longer storage.
11. Enjoy these delicious and nutritious muffins as a snack or a quick breakfast to support lactation!

Spinach and Mushroom Frittata

Ingredients:

- 8 large eggs
- 1/4 cup milk (dairy or plant-based)
- 1 tablespoon olive oil
- 1 small onion, diced
- 2 cups sliced mushrooms
- 2 cups fresh spinach leaves
- 1/2 cup shredded cheese (such as cheddar or mozzarella)
- Salt and black pepper, to taste
- Fresh herbs, such as parsley or thyme, for garnish (optional)

Instructions:

1. Preheat your oven to 350°F (175°C).
2. In a large mixing bowl, whisk together the eggs and milk until well combined. Season with salt and black pepper to taste. Set aside.
3. Heat the olive oil in a large oven-safe skillet over medium heat.
4. Add the diced onion to the skillet and sauté until softened and translucent, about 3-4 minutes.
5. Add the sliced mushrooms to the skillet and cook until they release their moisture and start to brown, about 5-6 minutes.
6. Add the fresh spinach leaves to the skillet and cook until wilted, about 2-3 minutes.
7. Spread the mushroom and spinach mixture evenly in the skillet.
8. Pour the whisked eggs over the mushroom and spinach mixture in the skillet, ensuring they are evenly distributed.
9. Cook the frittata on the stovetop for 3-4 minutes, or until the edges start to set.
10. Sprinkle the shredded cheese evenly over the top of the frittata.
11. Transfer the skillet to the preheated oven and bake for 12-15 minutes, or until the frittata is set in the center and the top is golden brown.
12. Once cooked, remove the skillet from the oven and let the frittata cool slightly.
13. Garnish with fresh herbs, if desired, before slicing and serving.
14. Enjoy this delicious spinach and mushroom frittata as a nutritious breakfast, brunch, or light meal!

Lentil Soup with Barley and Kale

Ingredients:

- 1 cup green or brown lentils, rinsed and drained
- 1/2 cup pearl barley, rinsed and drained
- 1 tablespoon olive oil
- 1 onion, diced
- 2 carrots, diced
- 2 celery stalks, diced
- 3 cloves garlic, minced
- 6 cups vegetable broth
- 1 can (14 oz) diced tomatoes
- 2 cups chopped kale leaves
- 1 teaspoon dried thyme
- 1 teaspoon dried oregano
- Salt and black pepper, to taste
- Fresh parsley, chopped, for garnish (optional)
- Lemon wedges, for serving (optional)

Instructions:

1. In a large pot, heat the olive oil over medium heat.
2. Add the diced onion, carrots, and celery to the pot. Cook, stirring occasionally, until the vegetables are softened, about 5-7 minutes.
3. Add the minced garlic to the pot and cook for another 1-2 minutes, until fragrant.
4. Stir in the rinsed lentils and pearl barley, then pour in the vegetable broth and diced tomatoes with their juices.
5. Add the dried thyme and oregano to the pot. Season with salt and black pepper to taste.
6. Bring the soup to a boil, then reduce the heat to low, cover, and simmer for about 30-35 minutes, or until the lentils and barley are tender.
7. Stir in the chopped kale leaves and simmer for an additional 5 minutes, until the kale is wilted and tender.
8. Taste the soup and adjust seasoning if needed.

9. Ladle the lentil soup with barley and kale into bowls. Garnish with chopped fresh parsley, if desired, and serve with lemon wedges on the side for squeezing over the soup before eating.
10. Enjoy this hearty and nutritious lentil soup with barley and kale as a comforting meal on a chilly day!

Oatmeal Chocolate Chip Lactation Bars

Ingredients:

- 1/2 cup unsalted butter, melted
- 1/2 cup honey or maple syrup
- 2 eggs
- 1 teaspoon vanilla extract
- 1 1/2 cups old-fashioned rolled oats
- 1 cup all-purpose flour
- 1/4 cup brewer's yeast
- 1/4 cup ground flaxseed meal
- 1/2 teaspoon baking soda
- 1/2 teaspoon salt
- 1/2 cup chocolate chips
- 1/4 cup chopped nuts (optional)

Instructions:

1. Preheat your oven to 350°F (175°C). Grease a 9x9-inch baking pan or line it with parchment paper.
2. In a large mixing bowl, whisk together the melted butter and honey or maple syrup until well combined.
3. Add the eggs and vanilla extract to the bowl, and whisk until smooth.
4. In another bowl, combine the rolled oats, all-purpose flour, brewer's yeast, ground flaxseed meal, baking soda, and salt.
5. Gradually add the dry ingredients to the wet ingredients, stirring until well combined.
6. Fold in the chocolate chips and chopped nuts (if using) until evenly distributed throughout the batter.
7. Pour the batter into the prepared baking pan and spread it out evenly.
8. Bake in the preheated oven for 20-25 minutes, or until the bars are golden brown and set in the center.
9. Remove the baking pan from the oven and let the bars cool completely before slicing into squares or bars.
10. Once cooled, store the oatmeal chocolate chip lactation bars in an airtight container at room temperature for up to 1 week, or freeze for longer storage.

11. Enjoy these delicious and nutritious lactation bars as a convenient snack to support breastfeeding!

Almond Butter Banana Smoothie

Ingredients:

- 1 ripe banana
- 2 tablespoons almond butter
- 1 cup almond milk (or any milk of your choice)
- 1 tablespoon honey or maple syrup (optional, for sweetness)
- 1/2 teaspoon vanilla extract
- 1/4 teaspoon ground cinnamon (optional)
- Ice cubes (optional)

Instructions:

1. Peel the ripe banana and break it into chunks.
2. In a blender, combine the banana chunks, almond butter, almond milk, honey or maple syrup (if using), vanilla extract, and ground cinnamon (if using).
3. If desired, add a few ice cubes to the blender to make the smoothie colder and more refreshing.
4. Blend all the ingredients together until smooth and creamy, scraping down the sides of the blender as needed.
5. Taste the smoothie and adjust sweetness or flavorings if necessary, adding more honey, vanilla extract, or cinnamon to taste.
6. Once the smoothie reaches your desired consistency and taste, pour it into glasses and serve immediately.
7. Optionally, garnish with a sprinkle of cinnamon or a slice of banana on the rim of the glass.
8. Enjoy this delicious and nutritious almond butter banana smoothie as a satisfying breakfast or snack!

Sweet Potato and Lentil Curry

Ingredients:

- 1 tablespoon coconut oil or olive oil
- 1 onion, chopped
- 2 cloves garlic, minced
- 1 tablespoon ginger, minced
- 2 medium sweet potatoes, peeled and diced
- 1 cup dried red lentils, rinsed and drained
- 1 can (14 oz) coconut milk
- 2 cups vegetable broth
- 1 tablespoon curry powder
- 1 teaspoon ground turmeric
- 1 teaspoon ground cumin
- 1/2 teaspoon ground coriander
- 1/4 teaspoon cayenne pepper (optional, for heat)
- Salt and black pepper, to taste
- Fresh cilantro, chopped, for garnish
- Cooked rice or naan bread, for serving

Instructions:

1. Heat the coconut oil or olive oil in a large pot over medium heat.
2. Add the chopped onion to the pot and sauté until softened and translucent, about 5 minutes.
3. Stir in the minced garlic and ginger, and cook for another 1-2 minutes until fragrant.
4. Add the diced sweet potatoes and rinsed red lentils to the pot, and stir to combine.
5. Pour in the coconut milk and vegetable broth, and stir in the curry powder, ground turmeric, ground cumin, ground coriander, and cayenne pepper (if using).
6. Season with salt and black pepper to taste.
7. Bring the curry to a boil, then reduce the heat to low and cover the pot with a lid.
8. Simmer the curry for 20-25 minutes, or until the sweet potatoes are tender and the lentils are cooked through, stirring occasionally.

9. Once cooked, taste the curry and adjust seasoning if necessary, adding more salt, pepper, or spices as desired.
10. Serve the sweet potato and lentil curry hot, garnished with chopped fresh cilantro.
11. Enjoy the curry with cooked rice or naan bread for a delicious and satisfying meal!

Blueberry Lactation Pancakes

Ingredients:

- 1 cup all-purpose flour
- 2 tablespoons brewer's yeast
- 2 tablespoons ground flaxseed meal
- 2 tablespoons sugar
- 1 teaspoon baking powder
- 1/2 teaspoon baking soda
- 1/4 teaspoon salt
- 1 cup buttermilk (or 1 cup milk mixed with 1 tablespoon lemon juice or vinegar)
- 1 large egg
- 2 tablespoons melted butter or oil
- 1 teaspoon vanilla extract
- 1/2 cup fresh or frozen blueberries
- Butter or oil for cooking
- Maple syrup, for serving

Instructions:

1. In a large bowl, whisk together the all-purpose flour, brewer's yeast, ground flaxseed meal, sugar, baking powder, baking soda, and salt until well combined.
2. In a separate bowl, whisk together the buttermilk, egg, melted butter or oil, and vanilla extract until smooth.
3. Pour the wet ingredients into the dry ingredients and stir until just combined. Be careful not to overmix; it's okay if there are a few lumps in the batter.
4. Gently fold in the blueberries until evenly distributed throughout the batter.
5. Heat a non-stick skillet or griddle over medium heat and lightly grease with butter or oil.
6. Pour 1/4 cup of batter onto the skillet for each pancake. Cook until bubbles form on the surface of the pancake and the edges start to look set, about 2-3 minutes.
7. Flip the pancakes and cook for an additional 1-2 minutes on the other side, or until golden brown and cooked through.
8. Repeat with the remaining batter, greasing the skillet as needed between batches.
9. Serve the blueberry lactation pancakes warm, drizzled with maple syrup.

10. Enjoy these delicious and nutritious pancakes as a comforting breakfast or snack to support lactation!

Salmon and Spinach Omelette

Ingredients:

- 2 large eggs
- 1 tablespoon milk or water
- Salt and pepper, to taste
- 1 teaspoon olive oil or butter
- 1/4 cup cooked salmon, flaked
- 1 cup fresh spinach leaves
- 2 tablespoons shredded cheese (such as cheddar or mozzarella), optional
- Chopped fresh herbs, such as dill or parsley, for garnish (optional)

Instructions:

1. In a small bowl, whisk together the eggs and milk or water until well combined. Season with salt and pepper to taste.
2. Heat the olive oil or butter in a non-stick skillet over medium heat.
3. Pour the egg mixture into the skillet, swirling it around to evenly coat the bottom.
4. Allow the eggs to cook undisturbed for a minute or two, until the edges start to set.
5. Using a spatula, gently lift the edges of the omelette and tilt the skillet to let the uncooked eggs flow underneath.
6. When the omelette is mostly set but still slightly runny on top, scatter the flaked salmon and fresh spinach leaves over one half of the omelette.
7. If using, sprinkle the shredded cheese over the salmon and spinach.
8. Carefully fold the other half of the omelette over the filling, creating a half-moon shape.
9. Cook for another minute or two, until the cheese is melted and the omelette is cooked through.
10. Slide the omelette onto a plate and garnish with chopped fresh herbs, if desired.
11. Serve the salmon and spinach omelette hot, with toast or a side salad if desired.
12. Enjoy this flavorful and protein-packed omelette for breakfast, brunch, or a quick and satisfying meal!

Pumpkin Spice Lactation Muffins

Ingredients:

- 1 3/4 cups all-purpose flour
- 1/2 cup brewer's yeast
- 1/4 cup ground flaxseed meal
- 1 teaspoon baking powder
- 1/2 teaspoon baking soda
- 1/2 teaspoon salt
- 1 teaspoon ground cinnamon
- 1/2 teaspoon ground ginger
- 1/4 teaspoon ground nutmeg
- 1/4 teaspoon ground cloves
- 1 cup pumpkin puree
- 1/2 cup coconut oil or melted butter
- 1/2 cup honey or maple syrup
- 2 large eggs
- 1 teaspoon vanilla extract
- 1/2 cup chopped nuts or chocolate chips (optional)

Instructions:

1. Preheat your oven to 350°F (175°C). Grease a muffin tin or line it with paper liners.
2. In a large bowl, whisk together the all-purpose flour, brewer's yeast, ground flaxseed meal, baking powder, baking soda, salt, cinnamon, ginger, nutmeg, and cloves until well combined.
3. In another bowl, mix together the pumpkin puree, coconut oil or melted butter, honey or maple syrup, eggs, and vanilla extract until smooth.
4. Pour the wet ingredients into the dry ingredients and stir until just combined. Be careful not to overmix; it's okay if there are a few lumps in the batter.
5. If using, fold in the chopped nuts or chocolate chips until evenly distributed throughout the batter.
6. Divide the batter evenly among the muffin cups, filling each about 2/3 full.
7. Bake in the preheated oven for 18-20 minutes, or until a toothpick inserted into the center of a muffin comes out clean.

8. Remove the muffins from the oven and let them cool in the muffin tin for 5 minutes before transferring them to a wire rack to cool completely.
9. Once cooled, store the pumpkin spice lactation muffins in an airtight container at room temperature for up to 3 days, or freeze for longer storage.
10. Enjoy these delicious and nutritious muffins as a convenient snack to support breastfeeding!

Spinach and Ricotta Stuffed Shells

Ingredients:

- 20 jumbo pasta shells
- 2 cups ricotta cheese
- 1 cup grated Parmesan cheese, divided
- 1 large egg
- 1 teaspoon dried oregano
- 1 teaspoon dried basil
- 1/2 teaspoon garlic powder
- Salt and pepper, to taste
- 1 cup chopped fresh spinach
- 2 cups marinara sauce
- Fresh basil leaves, chopped, for garnish (optional)

Instructions:

1. Preheat your oven to 375°F (190°C). Grease a 9x13-inch baking dish with olive oil or cooking spray.
2. Cook the jumbo pasta shells according to the package instructions until al dente. Drain and set aside to cool.
3. In a large mixing bowl, combine the ricotta cheese, 1/2 cup of grated Parmesan cheese, egg, dried oregano, dried basil, garlic powder, salt, and pepper. Mix until well combined.
4. Fold in the chopped fresh spinach until evenly distributed throughout the ricotta mixture.
5. Spoon a thin layer of marinara sauce onto the bottom of the prepared baking dish.
6. Stuff each cooked pasta shell with a generous spoonful of the spinach and ricotta mixture and place it in the baking dish.
7. Once all the shells are stuffed and arranged in the baking dish, spoon the remaining marinara sauce over the top of the shells.
8. Sprinkle the remaining 1/2 cup of grated Parmesan cheese over the sauce.
9. Cover the baking dish with aluminum foil and bake in the preheated oven for 25-30 minutes, or until the shells are heated through and the sauce is bubbling.

10. Remove the foil and bake for an additional 5-10 minutes, or until the cheese is melted and lightly golden brown.
11. Garnish with chopped fresh basil leaves, if desired, before serving.
12. Enjoy these delicious spinach and ricotta stuffed shells as a comforting and satisfying meal!

Apricot and Almond Lactation Bites

Ingredients:

- 1 cup old-fashioned rolled oats
- 1/2 cup almond butter
- 1/4 cup honey or maple syrup
- 1/4 cup ground flaxseed meal
- 1/4 cup brewer's yeast
- 1/2 cup chopped dried apricots
- 1/4 cup chopped almonds
- 1 teaspoon vanilla extract
- Pinch of salt

Instructions:

1. In a large mixing bowl, combine the old-fashioned rolled oats, almond butter, honey or maple syrup, ground flaxseed meal, brewer's yeast, chopped dried apricots, chopped almonds, vanilla extract, and a pinch of salt. Mix until well combined.
2. Cover the bowl and refrigerate the mixture for 30 minutes to allow it to firm up slightly.
3. Once chilled, use a small cookie scoop or spoon to portion out the mixture and roll it into bite-sized balls using your hands.
4. Place the formed lactation bites on a baking sheet lined with parchment paper.
5. Refrigerate the lactation bites for at least 1 hour, or until firm.
6. Once firm, transfer the lactation bites to an airtight container and store them in the refrigerator for up to 1 week, or freeze for longer storage.
7. Enjoy these apricot and almond lactation bites as a convenient and nutritious snack to support breastfeeding!

Chicken and Vegetable Stir-Fry

Ingredients:

- 2 boneless, skinless chicken breasts, thinly sliced
- 2 tablespoons soy sauce
- 1 tablespoon oyster sauce
- 1 tablespoon hoisin sauce
- 1 teaspoon sesame oil
- 2 tablespoons vegetable oil, divided
- 3 cloves garlic, minced
- 1 tablespoon minced ginger
- 1 onion, sliced
- 1 bell pepper, sliced
- 1 cup broccoli florets
- 1 cup sliced carrots
- 1 cup snap peas
- Salt and pepper, to taste
- Cooked rice or noodles, for serving
- Sesame seeds, for garnish (optional)
- Chopped green onions, for garnish (optional)

Instructions:

1. In a small bowl, combine the soy sauce, oyster sauce, hoisin sauce, and sesame oil. Stir well and set aside.
2. Heat 1 tablespoon of vegetable oil in a large skillet or wok over medium-high heat.
3. Add the sliced chicken breasts to the skillet and stir-fry for 3-4 minutes, or until cooked through. Remove the chicken from the skillet and set aside.
4. In the same skillet, add the remaining tablespoon of vegetable oil.
5. Add the minced garlic and ginger to the skillet and stir-fry for 1 minute, or until fragrant.
6. Add the sliced onion, bell pepper, broccoli florets, sliced carrots, and snap peas to the skillet. Stir-fry for 5-6 minutes, or until the vegetables are tender-crisp.
7. Return the cooked chicken to the skillet and pour the sauce over the chicken and vegetables. Stir well to coat everything evenly.

8. Cook for another 1-2 minutes, or until the sauce is heated through and everything is well combined.
9. Season with salt and pepper to taste.
10. Serve the chicken and vegetable stir-fry hot over cooked rice or noodles.
11. Garnish with sesame seeds and chopped green onions, if desired.
12. Enjoy this delicious and nutritious chicken and vegetable stir-fry as a flavorful meal!

Raspberry Chia Seed Pudding

Ingredients:

- 1/4 cup chia seeds
- 1 cup almond milk (or any milk of your choice)
- 1 tablespoon maple syrup or honey (optional, adjust to taste)
- 1/2 teaspoon vanilla extract
- 1/2 cup fresh or frozen raspberries
- Fresh raspberries, for garnish (optional)
- Mint leaves, for garnish (optional)

Instructions:

1. In a bowl or jar, combine the chia seeds, almond milk, maple syrup or honey (if using), and vanilla extract. Stir well to combine.
2. Let the mixture sit for 5 minutes, then stir again to prevent clumping.
3. Cover the bowl or jar and refrigerate for at least 2 hours, or preferably overnight, to allow the chia seeds to thicken and absorb the liquid.
4. In a blender or food processor, blend the raspberries until smooth.
5. Once the chia seed pudding has set, remove it from the refrigerator.
6. To assemble, layer the chia seed pudding and raspberry puree in serving glasses or jars.
7. Garnish with fresh raspberries and mint leaves, if desired.
8. Serve the raspberry chia seed pudding chilled.
9. Enjoy this refreshing and nutritious pudding as a breakfast, snack, or dessert!

Peanut Butter Lactation Energy Balls

Ingredients:

- 1 cup old-fashioned rolled oats
- 1/2 cup creamy peanut butter
- 1/4 cup honey or maple syrup
- 1/4 cup ground flaxseed meal
- 1/4 cup brewer's yeast
- 1 teaspoon vanilla extract
- Pinch of salt
- 1/2 cup mini chocolate chips (optional)
- 1/4 cup chopped nuts (such as almonds or walnuts) (optional)
- Shredded coconut, for rolling (optional)

Instructions:

1. In a large mixing bowl, combine the old-fashioned rolled oats, creamy peanut butter, honey or maple syrup, ground flaxseed meal, brewer's yeast, vanilla extract, and a pinch of salt. Mix until well combined.
2. If using, fold in the mini chocolate chips and chopped nuts until evenly distributed throughout the mixture.
3. Cover the bowl and refrigerate the mixture for 30 minutes to allow it to firm up slightly.
4. Once chilled, use a small cookie scoop or spoon to portion out the mixture and roll it into bite-sized balls using your hands.
5. If desired, roll the balls in shredded coconut for extra flavor and texture.
6. Place the formed energy balls on a baking sheet lined with parchment paper.
7. Refrigerate the energy balls for at least 1 hour, or until firm.
8. Once firm, transfer the energy balls to an airtight container and store them in the refrigerator for up to 1 week, or freeze for longer storage.
9. Enjoy these peanut butter lactation energy balls as a convenient and nutritious snack to support breastfeeding!

Vegetable and Bean Chili

Ingredients:

- 2 tablespoons olive oil
- 1 onion, diced
- 3 cloves garlic, minced
- 1 bell pepper, diced (any color)
- 2 carrots, diced
- 2 stalks celery, diced
- 1 zucchini, diced
- 1 yellow squash, diced
- 1 can (15 oz) kidney beans, drained and rinsed
- 1 can (15 oz) black beans, drained and rinsed
- 1 can (15 oz) diced tomatoes
- 1 cup vegetable broth
- 2 tablespoons tomato paste
- 1 tablespoon chili powder
- 1 teaspoon ground cumin
- 1 teaspoon paprika
- 1/2 teaspoon dried oregano
- Salt and pepper, to taste
- Chopped fresh cilantro or parsley, for garnish (optional)
- Sour cream or Greek yogurt, for serving (optional)
- Shredded cheese, for serving (optional)
- Sliced avocado, for serving (optional)
- Lime wedges, for serving (optional)

Instructions:

1. Heat the olive oil in a large pot over medium heat.
2. Add the diced onion and minced garlic to the pot. Cook, stirring occasionally, until the onion is softened and translucent, about 5 minutes.
3. Add the diced bell pepper, carrots, celery, zucchini, and yellow squash to the pot. Cook, stirring occasionally, for another 5 minutes, or until the vegetables start to soften.

4. Stir in the drained and rinsed kidney beans, black beans, diced tomatoes, vegetable broth, tomato paste, chili powder, ground cumin, paprika, dried oregano, salt, and pepper.
5. Bring the chili to a simmer, then reduce the heat to low and cover the pot with a lid.
6. Let the chili simmer for 20-25 minutes, stirring occasionally, or until the vegetables are tender and the flavors have melded together.
7. Taste the chili and adjust seasoning if necessary, adding more salt and pepper as needed.
8. Serve the vegetable and bean chili hot, garnished with chopped fresh cilantro or parsley if desired.
9. Optional: Serve with a dollop of sour cream or Greek yogurt, shredded cheese, sliced avocado, and lime wedges on the side.
10. Enjoy this hearty and flavorful vegetable and bean chili as a comforting meal!

Apple Cinnamon Lactation Muffins

Ingredients:

- 2 cups old-fashioned rolled oats
- 1 cup all-purpose flour
- 1/2 cup brewer's yeast
- 1/4 cup ground flaxseed meal
- 1 teaspoon baking powder
- 1/2 teaspoon baking soda
- 1/2 teaspoon salt
- 1 teaspoon ground cinnamon
- 1/2 cup unsweetened applesauce
- 1/2 cup maple syrup or honey
- 1/2 cup melted coconut oil or vegetable oil
- 2 large eggs
- 1 teaspoon vanilla extract
- 1 cup grated apple (about 1 medium apple)
- 1/2 cup chopped nuts (such as walnuts or pecans), optional

Instructions:

1. Preheat your oven to 350°F (175°C). Grease or line a muffin tin with paper liners.
2. In a large mixing bowl, combine the old-fashioned rolled oats, all-purpose flour, brewer's yeast, ground flaxseed meal, baking powder, baking soda, salt, and ground cinnamon. Mix until well combined.
3. In another bowl, whisk together the unsweetened applesauce, maple syrup or honey, melted coconut oil or vegetable oil, eggs, and vanilla extract until smooth.
4. Pour the wet ingredients into the dry ingredients and stir until just combined. Be careful not to overmix; it's okay if there are a few lumps in the batter.
5. Fold in the grated apple and chopped nuts (if using) until evenly distributed throughout the batter.
6. Divide the batter evenly among the muffin cups, filling each about 3/4 full.
7. Bake in the preheated oven for 18-20 minutes, or until a toothpick inserted into the center of a muffin comes out clean.
8. Remove the muffins from the oven and let them cool in the muffin tin for 5 minutes before transferring them to a wire rack to cool completely.

9. Once cooled, store the apple cinnamon lactation muffins in an airtight container at room temperature for up to 3 days, or freeze for longer storage.
10. Enjoy these delicious and nutritious muffins as a convenient snack to support breastfeeding!

Greek Yogurt Parfait with Berries

Ingredients:

- 1 cup Greek yogurt (plain or vanilla)
- 1/2 cup granola
- 1/2 cup mixed berries (such as strawberries, blueberries, raspberries)
- 1 tablespoon honey or maple syrup (optional)
- Fresh mint leaves, for garnish (optional)

Instructions:

1. In a serving glass or bowl, layer half of the Greek yogurt.
2. Sprinkle half of the granola over the yogurt layer.
3. Add half of the mixed berries on top of the granola.
4. Repeat the layers with the remaining Greek yogurt, granola, and mixed berries.
5. Drizzle honey or maple syrup over the top of the parfait, if desired, for extra sweetness.
6. Garnish with fresh mint leaves for a pop of color and flavor, if using.
7. Serve immediately and enjoy this delicious and nutritious Greek yogurt parfait with berries as a breakfast, snack, or dessert!

Tofu and Vegetable Stir-Fry

Ingredients:

- 14 oz (400g) firm tofu, drained and cubed
- 2 tablespoons soy sauce
- 1 tablespoon hoisin sauce
- 1 tablespoon sesame oil
- 2 tablespoons vegetable oil, divided
- 2 cloves garlic, minced
- 1 tablespoon minced ginger
- 1 onion, sliced
- 1 bell pepper, sliced (any color)
- 1 carrot, sliced
- 1 cup broccoli florets
- 1 cup snap peas
- Salt and pepper, to taste
- Cooked rice or noodles, for serving
- Sesame seeds, for garnish (optional)
- Chopped green onions, for garnish (optional)

Instructions:

1. In a bowl, combine the cubed tofu, soy sauce, hoisin sauce, and sesame oil. Toss until the tofu is evenly coated with the sauce mixture. Set aside to marinate for 10-15 minutes.
2. Heat 1 tablespoon of vegetable oil in a large skillet or wok over medium-high heat.
3. Add the marinated tofu to the skillet and cook for 5-7 minutes, stirring occasionally, until the tofu is golden brown and slightly crispy. Remove the tofu from the skillet and set aside.
4. In the same skillet, heat the remaining tablespoon of vegetable oil over medium heat.
5. Add the minced garlic and ginger to the skillet and cook for 1 minute, until fragrant.
6. Add the sliced onion, bell pepper, carrot, broccoli florets, and snap peas to the skillet. Stir-fry for 5-7 minutes, or until the vegetables are tender-crisp.

7. Return the cooked tofu to the skillet and toss with the vegetables.
8. Season with salt and pepper to taste.
9. Serve the tofu and vegetable stir-fry hot over cooked rice or noodles.
10. Garnish with sesame seeds and chopped green onions, if desired.
11. Enjoy this flavorful and nutritious tofu and vegetable stir-fry as a satisfying meal!

Chocolate Avocado Lactation Smoothie

Ingredients:

- 1 ripe avocado, peeled and pitted
- 1 ripe banana
- 2 tablespoons unsweetened cocoa powder
- 1 tablespoon ground flaxseed meal
- 1 tablespoon brewer's yeast
- 1 tablespoon honey or maple syrup (optional)
- 1 cup almond milk (or any milk of your choice)
- Ice cubes (optional)

Instructions:

1. In a blender, combine the ripe avocado, banana, unsweetened cocoa powder, ground flaxseed meal, brewer's yeast, honey or maple syrup (if using), and almond milk.
2. If desired, add a few ice cubes to the blender to make the smoothie colder and more refreshing.
3. Blend all the ingredients together until smooth and creamy, scraping down the sides of the blender as needed.
4. Taste the smoothie and adjust sweetness if necessary, adding more honey or maple syrup to taste.
5. Once the smoothie reaches your desired consistency and taste, pour it into glasses and serve immediately.
6. Optionally, garnish with a sprinkle of cocoa powder or a slice of avocado on the rim of the glass.
7. Enjoy this delicious and nutritious chocolate avocado lactation smoothie as a satisfying snack to support breastfeeding!

Quinoa and Black Bean Salad

Ingredients:

- 1 cup quinoa, rinsed
- 2 cups water or vegetable broth
- 1 can (15 oz) black beans, drained and rinsed
- 1 red bell pepper, diced
- 1 cup cherry tomatoes, halved
- 1/2 cup red onion, finely chopped
- 1/4 cup fresh cilantro, chopped
- 1/4 cup lime juice (about 2 limes)
- 2 tablespoons olive oil
- 1 teaspoon ground cumin
- 1/2 teaspoon chili powder
- Salt and pepper, to taste
- Avocado slices, for garnish (optional)

Instructions:

1. In a medium saucepan, combine the rinsed quinoa and water or vegetable broth. Bring to a boil, then reduce the heat to low, cover, and simmer for 15-20 minutes, or until the quinoa is cooked and the liquid is absorbed.
2. Once cooked, fluff the quinoa with a fork and let it cool to room temperature.
3. In a large mixing bowl, combine the cooked quinoa, black beans, diced red bell pepper, cherry tomatoes, chopped red onion, and chopped cilantro.
4. In a small bowl, whisk together the lime juice, olive oil, ground cumin, chili powder, salt, and pepper to make the dressing.
5. Pour the dressing over the quinoa and black bean mixture, and toss until everything is well coated.
6. Taste and adjust seasoning if necessary, adding more salt and pepper to taste.
7. Refrigerate the quinoa and black bean salad for at least 30 minutes to allow the flavors to meld together.
8. Before serving, garnish with avocado slices if desired.
9. Serve the quinoa and black bean salad chilled as a refreshing and nutritious side dish or main course. Enjoy!

Spinach and Cheese Quesadillas

Ingredients:

- 4 large flour tortillas
- 2 cups baby spinach leaves
- 1 cup shredded cheese (such as cheddar, Monterey Jack, or Mexican blend)
- 1/2 cup diced tomatoes (optional)
- 1/4 cup diced red onion (optional)
- 1/4 cup sliced black olives (optional)
- 1/4 teaspoon garlic powder
- Salt and pepper, to taste
- Olive oil or cooking spray, for cooking
- Salsa, sour cream, or guacamole, for serving (optional)

Instructions:

1. Place one flour tortilla on a flat surface.
2. Layer half of the spinach leaves evenly over one half of the tortilla.
3. Sprinkle half of the shredded cheese over the spinach leaves.
4. If using, distribute the diced tomatoes, diced red onion, and sliced black olives evenly over the cheese.
5. Sprinkle the garlic powder, salt, and pepper over the toppings.
6. Fold the other half of the tortilla over the filling to create a half-moon shape.
7. Repeat the process with the remaining tortillas and filling ingredients.
8. Heat a large skillet or griddle over medium heat. Lightly grease with olive oil or cooking spray.
9. Carefully place one quesadilla in the skillet and cook for 2-3 minutes on each side, or until golden brown and the cheese is melted.
10. Repeat with the remaining quesadillas.
11. Once cooked, remove the quesadillas from the skillet and let them cool for a minute before slicing into wedges.
12. Serve the spinach and cheese quesadillas hot, with salsa, sour cream, or guacamole on the side for dipping if desired.
13. Enjoy these delicious and flavorful quesadillas as a quick and satisfying meal or snack!

Chickpea and Sweet Potato Curry

Ingredients:

- 2 tablespoons olive oil
- 1 onion, diced
- 3 cloves garlic, minced
- 1 tablespoon minced ginger
- 2 medium sweet potatoes, peeled and diced
- 1 can (15 oz) chickpeas, drained and rinsed
- 1 can (14 oz) diced tomatoes
- 1 can (14 oz) coconut milk
- 2 teaspoons curry powder
- 1 teaspoon ground cumin
- 1 teaspoon ground turmeric
- 1/2 teaspoon ground coriander
- 1/4 teaspoon cayenne pepper (optional, for heat)
- Salt and pepper, to taste
- Fresh cilantro, chopped, for garnish
- Cooked rice or naan bread, for serving

Instructions:

1. Heat the olive oil in a large pot or skillet over medium heat.
2. Add the diced onion to the pot and cook for 3-4 minutes, or until softened and translucent.
3. Stir in the minced garlic and minced ginger, and cook for an additional 1-2 minutes, until fragrant.
4. Add the diced sweet potatoes to the pot and cook for 5 minutes, stirring occasionally.
5. Add the drained and rinsed chickpeas, diced tomatoes (with their juices), coconut milk, curry powder, ground cumin, ground turmeric, ground coriander, and cayenne pepper (if using) to the pot. Stir to combine.
6. Bring the mixture to a simmer, then reduce the heat to low. Cover the pot and let the curry simmer for 15-20 minutes, or until the sweet potatoes are tender.
7. Season the curry with salt and pepper to taste, adjusting the seasoning as needed.

8. Serve the chickpea and sweet potato curry hot, garnished with chopped fresh cilantro.
9. Enjoy the curry over cooked rice or with naan bread for a delicious and satisfying meal!

Mango Coconut Lactation Popsicles

Ingredients:

- 1 cup mango chunks (fresh or frozen)
- 1 cup coconut milk
- 1 tablespoon ground flaxseed meal
- 1 tablespoon brewer's yeast
- 1 tablespoon honey or maple syrup (optional, for sweetness)

Instructions:

1. In a blender, combine the mango chunks, coconut milk, ground flaxseed meal, brewer's yeast, and honey or maple syrup (if using).
2. Blend until smooth and well combined, scraping down the sides of the blender as needed.
3. Taste the mixture and adjust sweetness if necessary, adding more honey or maple syrup to taste.
4. Once the mixture reaches your desired sweetness, pour it into popsicle molds, leaving a little space at the top for expansion.
5. Insert popsicle sticks into the molds.
6. Place the popsicle molds in the freezer and freeze for at least 4-6 hours, or until the popsicles are completely frozen.
7. Once frozen, remove the popsicles from the molds by running them under warm water for a few seconds.
8. Serve the mango coconut lactation popsicles immediately and enjoy as a refreshing and nutritious treat to support breastfeeding!

Turkey and Vegetable Meatballs

Ingredients:

- 1 pound ground turkey
- 1/2 cup grated zucchini
- 1/2 cup grated carrot
- 1/4 cup finely chopped onion
- 2 cloves garlic, minced
- 1/4 cup breadcrumbs
- 1 large egg
- 2 tablespoons chopped fresh parsley
- 1 teaspoon dried oregano
- 1/2 teaspoon dried basil
- 1/2 teaspoon salt
- 1/4 teaspoon black pepper
- Olive oil, for cooking

Instructions:

1. Preheat your oven to 400°F (200°C). Line a baking sheet with parchment paper or lightly grease with olive oil.
2. In a large mixing bowl, combine the ground turkey, grated zucchini, grated carrot, chopped onion, minced garlic, breadcrumbs, egg, chopped parsley, dried oregano, dried basil, salt, and black pepper. Mix until well combined.
3. Roll the mixture into meatballs, about 1 to 1.5 inches in diameter, and place them on the prepared baking sheet.
4. Lightly brush or drizzle the meatballs with olive oil.
5. Bake in the preheated oven for 15-20 minutes, or until the meatballs are cooked through and lightly browned on the outside.
6. Once cooked, remove the meatballs from the oven and let them cool slightly before serving.
7. Serve the turkey and vegetable meatballs with your favorite sauce, such as marinara sauce or barbecue sauce, and enjoy as a delicious and nutritious meal!

Blueberry Banana Lactation Smoothie

Ingredients:

- 1 ripe banana
- 1/2 cup blueberries (fresh or frozen)
- 1 tablespoon ground flaxseed meal
- 1 tablespoon brewer's yeast
- 1 tablespoon honey or maple syrup (optional)
- 1 cup almond milk (or any milk of your choice)
- Ice cubes (optional)

Instructions:

1. Peel the ripe banana and break it into chunks.
2. In a blender, combine the banana chunks, blueberries, ground flaxseed meal, brewer's yeast, honey or maple syrup (if using), and almond milk.
3. If desired, add a few ice cubes to the blender to make the smoothie colder and more refreshing.
4. Blend all the ingredients together until smooth and creamy, scraping down the sides of the blender as needed.
5. Taste the smoothie and adjust sweetness if necessary, adding more honey or maple syrup to taste.
6. Once the smoothie reaches your desired consistency and taste, pour it into glasses and serve immediately.
7. Enjoy this delicious and nutritious blueberry banana lactation smoothie as a satisfying snack to support breastfeeding!

Caprese Salad with Balsamic Glaze

Ingredients:

- 2 large tomatoes, sliced
- 1 (8 oz) ball fresh mozzarella cheese, sliced
- Fresh basil leaves
- Balsamic glaze
- Extra virgin olive oil
- Salt and pepper, to taste

Instructions:

1. Arrange the tomato slices and mozzarella slices alternately on a serving platter.
2. Tuck fresh basil leaves between the tomato and mozzarella slices.
3. Drizzle balsamic glaze and extra virgin olive oil over the top of the salad.
4. Sprinkle with salt and pepper to taste.
5. Serve immediately as a refreshing appetizer or side dish. Enjoy!

Lentil and Vegetable Soup

Ingredients:

- 1 cup dried lentils, rinsed and drained
- 6 cups vegetable broth or water
- 2 tablespoons olive oil
- 1 onion, chopped
- 2 carrots, diced
- 2 celery stalks, diced
- 2 cloves garlic, minced
- 1 can (14 oz) diced tomatoes
- 1 teaspoon ground cumin
- 1 teaspoon ground coriander
- 1/2 teaspoon smoked paprika
- 1/4 teaspoon red pepper flakes (optional)
- Salt and pepper, to taste
- 2 cups chopped spinach or kale
- Juice of 1 lemon
- Fresh parsley, chopped, for garnish

Instructions:

1. In a large pot, heat the olive oil over medium heat.
2. Add the chopped onion, diced carrots, and diced celery to the pot. Cook, stirring occasionally, for 5-7 minutes, or until the vegetables are softened.
3. Add the minced garlic to the pot and cook for an additional 1-2 minutes, until fragrant.
4. Stir in the rinsed lentils, diced tomatoes (with their juices), ground cumin, ground coriander, smoked paprika, red pepper flakes (if using), salt, and pepper.
5. Pour in the vegetable broth or water, and bring the mixture to a boil.
6. Reduce the heat to low, cover the pot, and let the soup simmer for 25-30 minutes, or until the lentils are tender.
7. Stir in the chopped spinach or kale and lemon juice. Cook for an additional 5 minutes, until the greens are wilted.
8. Taste the soup and adjust seasoning if necessary, adding more salt, pepper, or lemon juice to taste.
9. Serve the lentil and vegetable soup hot, garnished with fresh chopped parsley.

10. Enjoy this hearty and nutritious soup as a comforting meal!

Pumpkin Spice Lactation Latte

Ingredients:

- 1 cup milk (dairy or plant-based)
- 1 tablespoon ground flaxseed meal
- 1 tablespoon brewer's yeast
- 1 tablespoon pumpkin puree
- 1/2 teaspoon pumpkin pie spice (or a mixture of cinnamon, nutmeg, and cloves)
- 1 tablespoon honey or maple syrup (optional)
- 1 shot of espresso or 1/2 cup strong brewed coffee

Instructions:

1. In a small saucepan, heat the milk over medium-low heat until warm but not boiling.
2. Whisk in the ground flaxseed meal, brewer's yeast, pumpkin puree, and pumpkin pie spice until well combined.
3. If using, stir in the honey or maple syrup until dissolved.
4. Remove the saucepan from the heat and pour the mixture into a blender.
5. Blend the mixture on high speed until frothy.
6. Pour the espresso or brewed coffee into a mug.
7. Carefully pour the frothed milk mixture over the coffee.
8. Optionally, sprinkle a little extra pumpkin pie spice on top for garnish.
9. Serve the pumpkin spice lactation latte immediately and enjoy as a delicious and comforting drink to support breastfeeding!

Avocado Toast with Poached Egg

Ingredients:

- 2 slices whole grain bread
- 1 ripe avocado
- 2 eggs
- Salt and pepper, to taste
- Red pepper flakes (optional)
- Chopped fresh herbs (such as parsley or chives), for garnish (optional)

Instructions:

1. Toast the slices of whole grain bread until golden brown and crispy.
2. While the bread is toasting, prepare the avocado. Cut the avocado in half, remove the pit, and scoop the flesh into a bowl. Mash the avocado with a fork until smooth, or leave it slightly chunky if desired. Season with salt and pepper to taste.
3. Bring a pot of water to a gentle simmer over medium heat. Crack one egg into a small bowl or ramekin.
4. Using a spoon, create a gentle whirlpool in the simmering water. Carefully slide the egg into the center of the whirlpool. Repeat with the second egg.
5. Poach the eggs for 3-4 minutes, or until the whites are set but the yolks are still runny.
6. While the eggs are poaching, spread the mashed avocado evenly onto the toasted bread slices.
7. Once the eggs are cooked to your liking, remove them from the water using a slotted spoon and drain any excess water.
8. Place one poached egg on top of each avocado toast.
9. Season the eggs with salt, pepper, and red pepper flakes (if using).
10. Garnish with chopped fresh herbs, if desired.
11. Serve the avocado toast with poached egg immediately, and enjoy this delicious and nutritious breakfast or brunch option!

Chicken and Broccoli Casserole

Ingredients:

- 2 cups cooked chicken, shredded or diced
- 2 cups broccoli florets
- 1 cup cooked rice or quinoa
- 1 cup shredded cheddar cheese
- 1/2 cup diced onion
- 2 cloves garlic, minced
- 1 can (10.5 oz) condensed cream of chicken soup
- 1/2 cup sour cream or Greek yogurt
- 1/4 cup milk
- 1 tablespoon olive oil
- Salt and pepper, to taste
- 1/2 cup breadcrumbs (optional)
- 2 tablespoons melted butter (optional)

Instructions:

1. Preheat your oven to 350°F (175°C). Grease a 9x13 inch baking dish.
2. In a large skillet, heat the olive oil over medium heat. Add the diced onion and minced garlic, and sauté until softened and fragrant, about 2-3 minutes.
3. Add the broccoli florets to the skillet and cook for another 3-4 minutes, or until slightly tender.
4. In a large mixing bowl, combine the cooked chicken, cooked rice or quinoa, sautéed onion and garlic, cooked broccoli, shredded cheddar cheese, condensed cream of chicken soup, sour cream or Greek yogurt, and milk. Season with salt and pepper to taste, and mix until well combined.
5. Transfer the chicken and broccoli mixture to the prepared baking dish, spreading it out evenly.
6. If desired, sprinkle breadcrumbs evenly over the top of the casserole mixture, and drizzle with melted butter for extra crunch.
7. Cover the baking dish with foil and bake in the preheated oven for 25-30 minutes, or until the casserole is heated through and bubbly.
8. Remove the foil and bake for an additional 5-10 minutes, or until the top is golden brown and crispy.

9. Once cooked, remove the casserole from the oven and let it cool for a few minutes before serving.
10. Serve the chicken and broccoli casserole hot as a comforting and satisfying meal for lunch or dinner. Enjoy!

Almond Joy Lactation Bars

Ingredients:

- 1 cup old-fashioned rolled oats
- 1 cup shredded coconut (unsweetened)
- 1/2 cup almond butter
- 1/4 cup ground flaxseed meal
- 1/4 cup brewer's yeast
- 1/2 cup honey or maple syrup
- 1/2 cup chopped almonds
- 1/2 cup mini chocolate chips
- 1 teaspoon vanilla extract
- Pinch of salt

Instructions:

1. Preheat your oven to 350°F (175°C). Line an 8x8 inch baking dish with parchment paper, leaving some overhang on the sides for easy removal.
2. In a large mixing bowl, combine the old-fashioned rolled oats, shredded coconut, almond butter, ground flaxseed meal, brewer's yeast, honey or maple syrup, chopped almonds, mini chocolate chips, vanilla extract, and a pinch of salt. Mix until well combined.
3. Transfer the mixture to the prepared baking dish, and use a spatula or your hands to press it down evenly into the bottom of the dish.
4. Bake in the preheated oven for 15-20 minutes, or until the edges are golden brown and the mixture is set.
5. Remove the baking dish from the oven and let it cool completely in the pan.
6. Once cooled, lift the bars out of the pan using the parchment paper overhang, and place them on a cutting board.
7. Use a sharp knife to cut the bars into individual squares or rectangles.
8. Store the almond joy lactation bars in an airtight container at room temperature for up to a week, or in the refrigerator for longer storage.
9. Enjoy these delicious and nutritious bars as a convenient snack to support breastfeeding!

Vegetable and Lentil Curry

Ingredients:

- 1 cup dried lentils, rinsed and drained
- 4 cups vegetable broth or water
- 2 tablespoons olive oil
- 1 onion, diced
- 3 cloves garlic, minced
- 1 tablespoon minced ginger
- 2 carrots, diced
- 2 potatoes, peeled and diced
- 1 bell pepper, diced
- 1 zucchini, diced
- 1 can (14 oz) diced tomatoes
- 1 can (14 oz) coconut milk
- 2 tablespoons curry powder
- 1 teaspoon ground cumin
- 1 teaspoon ground coriander
- 1/2 teaspoon turmeric
- 1/4 teaspoon cayenne pepper (optional, for heat)
- Salt and pepper, to taste
- Fresh cilantro, chopped, for garnish
- Cooked rice or naan bread, for serving

Instructions:

1. In a large pot or Dutch oven, heat the olive oil over medium heat.
2. Add the diced onion to the pot and cook for 5-7 minutes, or until softened and translucent.
3. Stir in the minced garlic and minced ginger, and cook for an additional 1-2 minutes, until fragrant.
4. Add the diced carrots, potatoes, bell pepper, and zucchini to the pot. Cook for 5 minutes, stirring occasionally.
5. Stir in the rinsed lentils, diced tomatoes (with their juices), coconut milk, curry powder, ground cumin, ground coriander, turmeric, cayenne pepper (if using), salt, and pepper.
6. Pour in the vegetable broth or water, and bring the mixture to a boil.

7. Reduce the heat to low, cover the pot, and let the curry simmer for 25-30 minutes, or until the lentils and vegetables are tender.
8. Taste the curry and adjust seasoning if necessary, adding more salt, pepper, or curry powder to taste.
9. Serve the vegetable and lentil curry hot, garnished with chopped fresh cilantro.
10. Enjoy the curry over cooked rice or with naan bread for a delicious and satisfying meal!

Quinoa and Vegetable Stir-Fry

Ingredients:

- 1 cup quinoa, rinsed
- 2 cups water or vegetable broth
- 2 tablespoons olive oil
- 1 onion, sliced
- 2 cloves garlic, minced
- 1 bell pepper, sliced
- 1 carrot, julienned
- 1 zucchini, sliced
- 1 cup broccoli florets
- 1 cup snap peas
- 1/4 cup soy sauce or tamari
- 2 tablespoons rice vinegar
- 1 tablespoon sesame oil
- 1 tablespoon honey or maple syrup
- 1 teaspoon grated ginger
- 1 teaspoon cornstarch (optional, for thickening)
- Salt and pepper, to taste
- Sesame seeds, for garnish (optional)
- Chopped green onions, for garnish (optional)

Instructions:

1. In a medium saucepan, combine the rinsed quinoa and water or vegetable broth. Bring to a boil, then reduce the heat to low, cover, and simmer for 15-20 minutes, or until the quinoa is cooked and the liquid is absorbed. Fluff the quinoa with a fork and set aside.
2. In a small bowl, whisk together the soy sauce or tamari, rice vinegar, sesame oil, honey or maple syrup, grated ginger, and cornstarch (if using). Set aside.
3. Heat olive oil in a large skillet or wok over medium-high heat. Add the sliced onion and minced garlic, and sauté for 2-3 minutes until fragrant.
4. Add the bell pepper, carrot, zucchini, broccoli florets, and snap peas to the skillet. Stir-fry for 5-7 minutes, or until the vegetables are tender-crisp.

5. Pour the sauce mixture over the vegetables in the skillet. Stir well to coat the vegetables evenly.
6. Add the cooked quinoa to the skillet and toss everything together until well combined. Cook for an additional 2-3 minutes to heat through.
7. Taste and adjust seasoning with salt and pepper if needed.
8. Remove from heat and transfer the quinoa and vegetable stir-fry to serving plates.
9. Garnish with sesame seeds and chopped green onions, if desired.
10. Serve hot and enjoy this delicious and nutritious quinoa and vegetable stir-fry as a satisfying meal!

Chocolate Peanut Butter Lactation Shake

Ingredients:

- 1 ripe banana
- 2 tablespoons peanut butter
- 1 tablespoon ground flaxseed meal
- 1 tablespoon brewer's yeast
- 1 tablespoon cocoa powder
- 1 cup almond milk (or any milk of your choice)
- 1 teaspoon honey or maple syrup (optional)
- Ice cubes (optional)

Instructions:

1. Peel the ripe banana and break it into chunks.
2. In a blender, combine the banana chunks, peanut butter, ground flaxseed meal, brewer's yeast, cocoa powder, almond milk, and honey or maple syrup (if using).
3. If desired, add a few ice cubes to the blender to make the shake colder and more refreshing.
4. Blend all the ingredients together until smooth and creamy, scraping down the sides of the blender as needed.
5. Taste the shake and adjust sweetness if necessary, adding more honey or maple syrup to taste.
6. Once the shake reaches your desired consistency and taste, pour it into glasses and serve immediately.
7. Enjoy this delicious and nutritious chocolate peanut butter lactation shake as a satisfying snack to support breastfeeding!

Eggplant Parmesan

Ingredients:

- 2 medium eggplants, sliced into 1/4-inch rounds
- Salt
- 2 cups breadcrumbs (panko or Italian-style)
- 1 cup grated Parmesan cheese
- 2 eggs, beaten
- 1 cup all-purpose flour
- Olive oil, for frying
- 2 cups marinara sauce
- 2 cups shredded mozzarella cheese
- Fresh basil leaves, for garnish (optional)

Instructions:

1. Preheat your oven to 375°F (190°C). Lightly grease a 9x13 inch baking dish.
2. Place the sliced eggplant rounds in a colander and sprinkle generously with salt. Let them sit for about 30 minutes to draw out excess moisture. After 30 minutes, rinse the eggplant slices thoroughly under cold water and pat them dry with paper towels.
3. In three separate shallow bowls, place the beaten eggs, flour, and breadcrumbs mixed with grated Parmesan cheese.
4. Dip each eggplant slice into the flour, shaking off any excess. Then dip it into the beaten eggs, followed by the breadcrumb mixture, pressing gently to adhere. Repeat with the remaining eggplant slices.
5. Heat olive oil in a large skillet over medium heat. Working in batches, fry the breaded eggplant slices until golden brown on both sides, about 2-3 minutes per side. Add more olive oil to the skillet as needed for each batch. Once fried, transfer the eggplant slices to a paper towel-lined plate to drain any excess oil.
6. Spread a thin layer of marinara sauce on the bottom of the prepared baking dish. Arrange half of the fried eggplant slices in a single layer over the sauce. Top with another layer of marinara sauce and half of the shredded mozzarella cheese. Repeat with the remaining eggplant slices, marinara sauce, and mozzarella cheese.

7. Cover the baking dish with aluminum foil and bake in the preheated oven for 25 minutes.
8. Remove the foil and bake for an additional 10-15 minutes, or until the cheese is melted and bubbly and the edges are golden brown.
9. Once cooked, remove the eggplant Parmesan from the oven and let it cool for a few minutes before serving.
10. Garnish with fresh basil leaves, if desired, and serve hot. Enjoy this classic Italian dish as a delicious and comforting meal!

Banana Walnut Lactation Bread

Ingredients:

- 2 ripe bananas, mashed
- 2 eggs
- 1/2 cup coconut oil, melted (or any oil of your choice)
- 1/4 cup honey or maple syrup
- 1 teaspoon vanilla extract
- 1/2 cup almond milk (or any milk of your choice)
- 1/4 cup ground flaxseed meal
- 1/4 cup brewer's yeast
- 1 3/4 cups all-purpose flour
- 1 teaspoon baking powder
- 1/2 teaspoon baking soda
- 1/2 teaspoon ground cinnamon
- 1/4 teaspoon salt
- 1/2 cup chopped walnuts

Instructions:

1. Preheat your oven to 350°F (175°C). Grease a 9x5 inch loaf pan or line it with parchment paper.
2. In a large mixing bowl, combine the mashed bananas, eggs, melted coconut oil, honey or maple syrup, vanilla extract, and almond milk. Mix until well combined.
3. Stir in the ground flaxseed meal and brewer's yeast until fully incorporated into the wet ingredients.
4. In a separate bowl, whisk together the all-purpose flour, baking powder, baking soda, ground cinnamon, and salt.
5. Gradually add the dry ingredients to the wet ingredients, mixing until just combined. Be careful not to overmix.
6. Fold in the chopped walnuts until evenly distributed throughout the batter.
7. Pour the batter into the prepared loaf pan, smoothing the top with a spatula.
8. Bake in the preheated oven for 50-60 minutes, or until a toothpick inserted into the center comes out clean.
9. If the top of the bread begins to brown too quickly, loosely tent it with aluminum foil.

10. Once baked, remove the bread from the oven and let it cool in the pan for 10 minutes before transferring it to a wire rack to cool completely.
11. Once cooled, slice and serve the banana walnut lactation bread. Enjoy it as a delicious and nutritious snack to support breastfeeding!

Greek Salad with Grilled Chicken

Ingredients:

For the Salad:

- 2 boneless, skinless chicken breasts
- Salt and pepper, to taste
- 1 tablespoon olive oil
- 1 head romaine lettuce, chopped
- 1 cucumber, diced
- 1 cup cherry tomatoes, halved
- 1/2 red onion, thinly sliced
- 1/2 cup Kalamata olives, pitted
- 1/2 cup crumbled feta cheese
- Fresh oregano leaves, for garnish (optional)

For the Dressing:

- 1/4 cup extra virgin olive oil
- 2 tablespoons red wine vinegar
- 1 teaspoon Dijon mustard
- 1 clove garlic, minced
- 1/2 teaspoon dried oregano
- Salt and pepper, to taste

Instructions:

1. Preheat a grill or grill pan over medium-high heat.
2. Season the chicken breasts with salt and pepper, then drizzle with olive oil.
3. Grill the chicken breasts for 6-8 minutes per side, or until cooked through and no longer pink in the center. Remove from the grill and let them rest for a few minutes before slicing.

4. Meanwhile, prepare the salad. In a large bowl, combine the chopped romaine lettuce, diced cucumber, halved cherry tomatoes, thinly sliced red onion, and pitted Kalamata olives.
5. In a small bowl or jar, whisk together the extra virgin olive oil, red wine vinegar, Dijon mustard, minced garlic, dried oregano, salt, and pepper to make the dressing.
6. Pour the dressing over the salad and toss until well coated.
7. Divide the salad among serving plates.
8. Slice the grilled chicken breasts and place them on top of each salad.
9. Sprinkle crumbled feta cheese over the salads.
10. Garnish with fresh oregano leaves, if desired.
11. Serve the Greek salad with grilled chicken immediately, and enjoy this flavorful and satisfying dish!

Lentil and Spinach Salad

Ingredients:

- 1 cup dried green or brown lentils
- 3 cups water or vegetable broth
- 4 cups fresh spinach leaves, washed and dried
- 1/2 cup cherry tomatoes, halved
- 1/4 cup red onion, thinly sliced
- 1/4 cup crumbled feta cheese (optional)
- 1/4 cup chopped fresh parsley

For the Dressing:

- 3 tablespoons extra virgin olive oil
- 2 tablespoons balsamic vinegar
- 1 teaspoon Dijon mustard
- 1 clove garlic, minced
- Salt and pepper, to taste

Instructions:

1. Rinse the lentils under cold water and drain.
2. In a medium saucepan, combine the rinsed lentils and water or vegetable broth. Bring to a boil over high heat, then reduce the heat to low and simmer, covered, for 20-25 minutes, or until the lentils are tender but still hold their shape. Drain any excess liquid and set aside to cool.
3. In a large mixing bowl, combine the cooked lentils, fresh spinach leaves, halved cherry tomatoes, thinly sliced red onion, crumbled feta cheese (if using), and chopped fresh parsley.
4. In a small bowl, whisk together the extra virgin olive oil, balsamic vinegar, Dijon mustard, minced garlic, salt, and pepper to make the dressing.
5. Pour the dressing over the lentil and spinach salad and toss until well combined and evenly coated.
6. Taste and adjust seasoning with more salt and pepper if needed.

7. Serve the salad immediately, or refrigerate for 30 minutes to allow the flavors to meld.
8. Enjoy this flavorful and nutritious lentil and spinach salad as a side dish or a light meal!

Mango Pineapple Lactation Smoothie

Ingredients:

- 1 cup frozen mango chunks
- 1 cup frozen pineapple chunks
- 1 ripe banana
- 1 tablespoon ground flaxseed meal
- 1 tablespoon brewer's yeast
- 1 cup almond milk (or any milk of your choice)
- 1/2 cup Greek yogurt
- 1 teaspoon honey or maple syrup (optional)

Instructions:

1. Place the frozen mango chunks, frozen pineapple chunks, ripe banana, ground flaxseed meal, brewer's yeast, almond milk, Greek yogurt, and honey or maple syrup (if using) in a blender.
2. Blend on high speed until smooth and creamy, scraping down the sides of the blender as needed.
3. If the smoothie is too thick, add more almond milk, a little at a time, until you reach your desired consistency.
4. Taste the smoothie and adjust sweetness if necessary by adding more honey or maple syrup.
5. Once blended to your liking, pour the smoothie into glasses and serve immediately.
6. Enjoy this delicious and refreshing mango pineapple lactation smoothie as a nutritious snack to support breastfeeding!

Tomato Basil Lactation Soup

Ingredients:

- 2 tablespoons olive oil
- 1 onion, chopped
- 2 cloves garlic, minced
- 4 cups vegetable broth
- 2 cans (14 oz each) diced tomatoes
- 1/4 cup tomato paste
- 1 teaspoon dried basil
- 1/2 teaspoon dried oregano
- 1/4 teaspoon red pepper flakes (optional, for heat)
- Salt and pepper, to taste
- 1/4 cup ground flaxseed meal
- 1/4 cup brewer's yeast
- 1/2 cup heavy cream or coconut cream (optional)
- Fresh basil leaves, chopped, for garnish (optional)

Instructions:

1. In a large pot, heat the olive oil over medium heat. Add the chopped onion and sauté until softened and translucent, about 5 minutes.
2. Add the minced garlic to the pot and cook for an additional minute until fragrant.
3. Pour in the vegetable broth, diced tomatoes (with their juices), and tomato paste. Stir to combine.
4. Add the dried basil, dried oregano, red pepper flakes (if using), salt, and pepper to the pot. Stir well and bring the soup to a simmer.
5. Let the soup simmer for about 20-25 minutes, stirring occasionally, to allow the flavors to meld.
6. Stir in the ground flaxseed meal and brewer's yeast. Simmer for an additional 5 minutes.
7. If using, stir in the heavy cream or coconut cream to add richness and creaminess to the soup.
8. Taste the soup and adjust seasoning if necessary, adding more salt and pepper as desired.

9. Once the soup is ready, ladle it into bowls and garnish with chopped fresh basil leaves, if desired.
10. Serve the tomato basil lactation soup hot, and enjoy its comforting and nourishing flavors!

Turkey and Avocado Wrap

Ingredients:

- 1 large whole wheat or spinach tortilla
- 3-4 slices of roasted turkey breast
- 1/2 avocado, sliced
- Handful of mixed greens (such as lettuce, spinach, or arugula)
- 1 tablespoon hummus or Greek yogurt
- 1 tablespoon Dijon mustard (optional)
- Salt and pepper, to taste

Instructions:

1. Lay the tortilla flat on a clean surface.
2. Spread the hummus or Greek yogurt evenly over the tortilla, leaving a small border around the edges.
3. If using, spread the Dijon mustard over the hummus or Greek yogurt.
4. Arrange the slices of roasted turkey breast on top of the hummus or Greek yogurt.
5. Place the sliced avocado on top of the turkey.
6. Season with salt and pepper, to taste.
7. Scatter the mixed greens over the avocado.
8. Starting from one end, tightly roll up the tortilla, enclosing the filling.
9. Secure the wrap with toothpicks if needed, then slice it in half diagonally.
10. Serve the turkey and avocado wrap immediately, or wrap it in parchment paper or aluminum foil for an on-the-go meal.
11. Enjoy this delicious and nutritious wrap for lunch or a light dinner!

Black Bean and Corn Salad

Ingredients:

- 1 can (15 oz) black beans, rinsed and drained
- 1 cup corn kernels (fresh, canned, or frozen)
- 1 red bell pepper, diced
- 1/2 red onion, finely chopped
- 1 jalapeño pepper, seeded and finely chopped (optional)
- 1/4 cup fresh cilantro, chopped
- Juice of 1 lime
- 2 tablespoons extra virgin olive oil
- 1 teaspoon ground cumin
- 1/2 teaspoon chili powder
- Salt and pepper, to taste
- Avocado slices, for serving (optional)
- Tortilla chips, for serving (optional)

Instructions:

1. In a large mixing bowl, combine the black beans, corn kernels, diced red bell pepper, finely chopped red onion, chopped jalapeño pepper (if using), and chopped fresh cilantro.
2. In a small bowl, whisk together the lime juice, extra virgin olive oil, ground cumin, chili powder, salt, and pepper to make the dressing.
3. Pour the dressing over the black bean and corn salad, and toss until well combined and evenly coated.
4. Taste and adjust seasoning with more salt and pepper if needed.
5. Cover the salad and refrigerate for at least 30 minutes to allow the flavors to meld.
6. Before serving, give the salad a final toss and garnish with avocado slices, if desired.
7. Serve the black bean and corn salad as a side dish, or enjoy it as a topping for tacos, quesadillas, or grilled meats.
8. Optionally, serve with tortilla chips on the side for scooping.
9. Enjoy this flavorful and refreshing salad as a delicious addition to your meal!

Lemon Blueberry Lactation Scones

Ingredients:

- 2 cups all-purpose flour
- 1/3 cup granulated sugar
- 1 tablespoon baking powder
- 1/2 teaspoon salt
- 1/2 cup cold unsalted butter, cut into small cubes
- Zest of 1 lemon
- 1/2 cup blueberries (fresh or frozen)
- 1/2 cup milk (regular or lactation-friendly milk)
- 1 large egg
- 1 teaspoon vanilla extract
- 1 tablespoon ground flaxseed meal
- 1 tablespoon brewer's yeast
- 1 tablespoon lemon juice

For the Glaze:

- 1 cup powdered sugar
- 2-3 tablespoons fresh lemon juice
- Zest of 1 lemon

Instructions:

1. Preheat your oven to 400°F (200°C). Line a baking sheet with parchment paper or silicone baking mat.
2. In a large mixing bowl, whisk together the flour, sugar, baking powder, and salt.
3. Add the cold cubed butter to the flour mixture. Using a pastry cutter or your fingertips, work the butter into the flour mixture until it resembles coarse crumbs with pea-sized butter pieces.
4. Stir in the lemon zest and blueberries until evenly distributed.
5. In a small bowl, whisk together the milk, egg, vanilla extract, ground flaxseed meal, brewer's yeast, and lemon juice until well combined.

6. Pour the wet ingredients over the dry ingredients. Using a spatula or wooden spoon, gently mix until the dough starts to come together. Be careful not to overmix.
7. Turn the dough out onto a lightly floured surface and gently knead it a few times until it comes together into a cohesive ball.
8. Pat the dough into a circle about 1 inch thick. Using a sharp knife or bench scraper, cut the circle into 8 wedges.
9. Transfer the scones to the prepared baking sheet, spacing them apart.
10. Bake in the preheated oven for 15-18 minutes, or until the scones are golden brown and cooked through.
11. While the scones are baking, prepare the glaze. In a small bowl, whisk together the powdered sugar, lemon juice, and lemon zest until smooth.
12. Once the scones are done baking, remove them from the oven and let them cool on the baking sheet for a few minutes.
13. Drizzle the glaze over the warm scones.
14. Allow the glaze to set for a few minutes before serving.
15. Serve the lemon blueberry lactation scones warm or at room temperature.
16. Enjoy these delicious scones as a treat during breastfeeding sessions!

Vegetable and Tofu Stir-Fry

Ingredients:

- 14 oz (400g) firm tofu, pressed and cubed
- 2 tablespoons soy sauce
- 1 tablespoon cornstarch
- 2 tablespoons vegetable oil
- 2 cloves garlic, minced
- 1 tablespoon ginger, minced
- 1 bell pepper, thinly sliced
- 1 carrot, julienned
- 1 cup broccoli florets
- 1 cup snap peas
- 1 cup sliced mushrooms
- 1/4 cup soy sauce (for stir-fry sauce)
- 2 tablespoons hoisin sauce
- 1 tablespoon rice vinegar
- 1 tablespoon sesame oil
- Cooked rice or noodles, for serving
- Sesame seeds and chopped green onions, for garnish (optional)

Instructions:

1. In a small bowl, mix together 2 tablespoons of soy sauce and cornstarch. Toss the cubed tofu in this mixture until coated.
2. Heat 1 tablespoon of vegetable oil in a large skillet or wok over medium-high heat. Add the tofu cubes and cook until golden brown on all sides, about 5-7 minutes. Remove the tofu from the skillet and set aside.
3. In the same skillet, add the remaining tablespoon of vegetable oil. Add the minced garlic and ginger, and cook for about 1 minute until fragrant.
4. Add the sliced bell pepper, julienned carrot, broccoli florets, snap peas, and sliced mushrooms to the skillet. Stir-fry for 5-7 minutes until the vegetables are tender-crisp.
5. In a small bowl, whisk together the remaining soy sauce, hoisin sauce, rice vinegar, and sesame oil to make the stir-fry sauce.

6. Return the cooked tofu to the skillet with the vegetables. Pour the stir-fry sauce over the tofu and vegetables, and toss everything together until evenly coated.
7. Cook for an additional 2-3 minutes until the sauce has thickened slightly and everything is heated through.
8. Serve the vegetable and tofu stir-fry hot over cooked rice or noodles.
9. Garnish with sesame seeds and chopped green onions, if desired.
10. Enjoy this delicious and nutritious vegetable and tofu stir-fry as a satisfying meal!